A MAXWELL WINSTON STONE SERIES

AND THE ANIMALS SHALL TEACH US

ANGELS IN DISGUISE

ERNIE CARWILE

A MAXWELL WINSTON STONE SERIES

AND THE ANIMALS SHALL TEACH US

ANGELS IN DISGUISE

ERNIE CARWILE

Verbena Pond Publishing Co., L.L.C.

For information, contact Verbena Pond Publishing Co., L.L.C., P.O. Box 370270, Denver, CO 80237. www.VerbenaPondPublishing.com, or 303-641-8632.

ISBN: 978-0-9796176-4-5

Library of congress Control Number: 2010926493

This book is dedicated to my late dog and pal, Tally-o-Mally, truly one of the angels in disguise.

OTHER BOOKS BY ERNIE CARWILE

ATTITUDE: It's Not What You See, It's How You See

CONNECTED BY THE SOUL: Oh, the Oneness of Us All

RECLAIMING THE POWER OF SILENCE

PERSISTENCE: The Art of Failing Until You Succeed

WHERE DO WE GO FROM HERE? Death, the Next Great Adventure

NEVER GOOD ENOUGH: Discover the Treasure of Self-Acceptance

CHIPPED BUT NOT BROKEN: When Adversity Enhances the Human Spirit

THE MAX CHRONICLES presents *THE STORYTELLER 1*

AND THE ANIMALS SHALL TEACH US:
Angels in Disguise

A FEW OF THE MANY ENDORSEMENTS/THANK YOU'S FOR THE MAXWELL WINSTON STONE SERIES

"I would like to take this opportunity to thank you for sending me **Attitude: It's Not What You See, It's How You See**...I wish you all of the best in your future endeavors."

—BARACK OBAMA
President of the United States

"Thank you very much for your book...It was 100% good stuff that we all need to absorb and live with."

—STEVE SPURRIER
Head Football Coach
University of South Carolina

"Some of the most spiritual yet realistic books of our time—they are phenomenal."

—DR. ROBERT CARROL

"I have always taught my children to look on the bright side of life—and your book on attitude expresses this concept perfectly."

—BILL OWENS
Governor of Colorado 1999–2007

"These books speak to the world. Everyone should read them."

—Edwin Alexander
Former Director of the Federal Home Loan Bank

"Thank you for your book on ATTITUDE. I'm adding it to my personal lending library at my office so my staff and others can read it, too."

—Governor Jennifer M. Granholm
State of Michigan

"There must be something BIGGER than the universe to brag about how much I enjoyed you and your books… How special they are and have definitely made a difference in my life."

—Debbie Wilden
President/CEO
Cottonwood Chamber of Commerce, AZ

"Your works are very inspirational and provide the readers with gems of wisdom on how to pursue a more positive and harmonious life. They are truly remarkable."

—Governor Anibal Acevedo Vila
Commonwealth of Puerto Rico

NTRODUCTION

If you have been following THE MAXWELL WINSTON STONE book series, you know that this is the eighth book in what will be a fifteen book series.

If you have not read any of the prior books, please note you do *not* have to read them in any particular order. In reading any of the others you will learn more about my friend, Max. Suffice it to say for now that he was someone who monumentally affected my life through a seemingly endless storehouse of stories and quotes which were all applicable to the life difficulties I was experiencing at that time. Never preachy, Max just had a knack for speaking simply and frankly to problems we humans get to deal with.

This new book, ***AND THE ANIMALS SHALL TEACH US: Angels in Disguise*** affected both Max and me just like the other books. We each have always sensed a special bond with animals and freely admitted that these wonderful creatures provided us with perhaps the only source of safety and acceptance we experienced growing up.

Remember that all of the topics in the MAXWELL WINSTON STONE SERIES were selected by researching quotes going back twenty-five hundred years to the time of Aristotle and Socrates. Those topics which received the most number of quotes became a separate book. So when I discovered that "animal quotes" were among the fifteen most quoted *life themes* throughout history, I easily sensed that it was my destiny to write about these magnificent creatures in this eighth book.

Animal stories and books have always been an intimate part of our culture. Do you remember the book, ***OLD YELLER***? I was nine or ten when I first read where Yeller had been exposed to a rabid wolf while defending the family. After realizing that Yeller had contracted the fatal disease, Travis, the young boy closest to Yeller, knew that the dog would have to be put down and that it was his responsibility to do so. I can still remember hiding in the closet with a pillow over my face in an attempt to keep anyone from hearing my wracking sobs after reading when young Travis shot Old Yeller.

The same with Jack London's book, ***THE CALL OF THE WILD***. At the end, after Buck's master had been killed by some Indians, the narrator said that Buck returned to visit his master's grave every year, never forgetting how much he loved him. Where was I? Again, hiding out in the closet with a pillow muffling my pitiful crying.

Other famous animal books that have withstood the forgetfulness of time include such best sellers as ***BLACK BEAUTY, WATERSHIP DOWN, ANIMAL FARM, MOBY DICK, THE INCREDIBLE JOURNEY, THE BIRD MAN OF ALCATRAZ, WHERE THE WILD THINGS ARE*** and then there was Marjorie Rawlings' ***THE YEARLING***.

I am sure there are other great animal books, but let's face it, people have written so much about animals/pets throughout time because they bring us much joy—a rare commodity in this sometimes cold and cruel world in which we live. They also teach us about the real and most important things in life, for example, attitude, friendship, unconditional love, loyalty, giving comfort when comfort is especially needed, forgiveness, how to deal with adversity, self-worth, generosity, trust, humor, courage, acceptance, values—AND they are gifted in so many areas of intelligence, most of which we are still in the process of discovering.

So sit back and enjoy what could very well be a **life-changing journey** into the realm of the animal kingdom. Let your imagination soar. As Albert Einstein wrote, "Imagination is more important than knowledge, for with imagination you can change reality."

If you think a dog can't count, try putting three dog biscuits in your pocket and give Fido only two of them.

—PHIL PASTORET
(ALIVE AND WELL)

PET PLEA

Treat me kindly, my beloved friend, for no heart in the entire world is more grateful for kindness than my loving heart.

Do not break my spirit with a stick, for though I should lick your hand between blows, your patience and understanding will more quickly teach me the things you would have me learn.

Speak to me often, for your voice is the world's sweetest music, as you must know by the fierce wagging of my tail when your footstep falls on my waiting ear.

Please take me inside when it is cold and wet, for I am a domesticated animal, no longer accustomed to the bitter elements. Nothing brings me greater joy than the privilege of sitting at your feet beside the hearth.

Keep my pan filled with fresh water, for I cannot tell you when I am thirsty.

Feed me clean food that I may stay well, to romp and play and do your bidding, to walk by your side, and stand ready, willing and able to protect you with my life, should your life be in danger.

And my friend, when I am very old, and I no longer enjoy good health, hearing and sight, do not make heroic efforts to keep me going. I am not having any fun. Please see that my trusting life is taken gently. I shall leave this earth knowing with the last breath I draw that my fate was always safest in your hands.

—Author Unknown

A dog is the only thing on earth that loves you more than he loves himself.

—Josh Billings
American Humorist
(1818–1885)

IF YOU COULD...

If you could love unconditionally,
If you could learn to forgive instantly,
If you could never judge anyone,
If you could take blame and
criticism without resentment,
If you could understand when you're loved
ones were too busy to spend time with you,
If you could relax without liquor,
If you could ignore a person's limited
education and never devalue them,
If you could live every day with abandonment,
If you could eat the same food every
day and be appreciative of it,
If you could face the world without
deceiving and lying,
If you could resist complaining,
If you could treat all people without regard
to their sex, culture or color of their skin,
If you could deal with stress without medical help,
If you could always maintain a happy disposition,
THEN YOU WOULD BE ALMOST
AS GOOD AS YOUR DOG.

—**Maxwell Winston Stone**

Who can believe there is no soul behind those luminous eyes?

—Theophile Gautier
French poet and Novelist
(1811–1872)

"God so loved the world and animals that He gave the mirror image of His name to the dog."

"HEY, ERNIE," MAX ASKED, "Do you think animals are spiritual?"

"Whoa," I said, "That's a pretty deep question." We were sitting in a park on a hot July afternoon enjoying the cool shade from an array of trees and feeding the hungry and curious squirrels. I just love these highly intelligent and emotional little creatures.

"Maybe so," Max persisted, "but what about it? Do you think animals are aware of God? And even better, do you think animals have spirits?"

One thing for sure, being around Max was always challenging.

"Actually Max, that's a good question," I admitted, "and I guess I do."

"Did you know that animals were once worshipped as gods and goddesses?" he asked further.

I nodded my head yes.

"Why would our ancestors attribute divinity to the animals?" Of course, he didn't even wait for a response from me, but just plunged right ahead.

"Because animals touch us in some deep center within our beings. Pet owners especially know this and appreciate the sense of wonder and joy of creation they bring."

Max had my complete attention now.

"Meister Eckhart, a German theologian and mystic way back in the thirteenth century presented the term 'funklein', which means that every human is born with a 'spark of divinity.' Then I read that the famous primatologist, Jane Goodall, said, 'I came to believe that all living things possess a spark of that Spiritual Power, this spark that we humans call our *soul*. And if this is so, it must surely be true for other animals.'"

Max continued, "Goodall cited the example of when an adult male chimpanzee comes upon a magnificent waterfall, the animal's hair bristles, a sign of heightened arousal. Furthermore, she said that as the animal comes closer to the waterfall and enters its connecting stream, it performs a kind of dance that can last up to ten minutes."

My mouth must have been open for Max reminded me to close it.

"Ernie, animals have also acted as our teachers throughout history. Remember Aesop's Fables?"

I again nodded, "Sure."

"Written five hundred years before Christ, they are a collection of animal stories that convey a moral lesson: like The Fox and the Grapes, which is where the term *sour grapes* originated; or, The Tortoise and the Hare, which taught us that it is not necessarily the fastest who wins the race, but the most persistent."

"I remember them, Max."

"But today, Ernie, something quite significant has changed. Just recently, our societies' respect for animals has shot upward and our concern for animals has risen exponentially. Remember back forty or fifty years ago when we had little concern about wild animals? I mean, safaris were the hip thing to do, monkeys and rats were experimented upon unrestrained and whales were slaughtered without any conscience. Now our safaris only allow *photographing* the wild animals, we have bans on killing the whales and there are protests galore to halt the cruel practice of animal experimentation."

After pausing a moment to allow this information to sink in, he followed up by asking, "Why has this change taken place? Does raising our consciousness require us to have a new respect for these animals with which we share our planet?"

See what I mean? Max's questions always jarred my brain into having new thoughts; forced me to move out of the familiar.

"Maybe, just maybe," Max spoke earnestly, "we have come to realize that our renewed interest and respect for animals is the key to ***us*** growing spiritually."

Max and I sat there in silence for the longest of time until our reverence was broken by some of his newest thoughts. "And another thing, most pet owners will attest that their animals *speak* to them but can't adequately explain how this is accomplished since words are not used. Wise persons have suggested that where animals don't talk like we do, they still communicate quite well. This *other way* of talking seems to remind us of some ancient remembrance that there are other levels of consciousness."

Max was getting worked up again.

"See, perhaps the greatest teaching we can learn from our animal friends is to be able to go beyond the boundaries of being just human. Maybe we are learning that they show us that other realms also exist, specifically the spiritual, the area which will enrich our lives beyond our wildest imaginings."

Completely caught up in Max's history lesson and insights, this one question bolted into my consciousness, *Could perhaps everything on our planet have a spirit?*

If I were more like my dog,
I'd be a better human being.

—Maxwell Winston Stone

"Thank you for never telling my secrets."

It simply amazes me that when you begin focusing on some topic, your mind filters out the other things so you focus more on that topic or object. For example, if you purchase a certain model of car, you suddenly begin seeing that model wherever you go. I think that portion of your brain that handles this is called, R.A.S., or reticular activating system.

In this case, Max and I had decided we would begin researching traits that animals exhibit which we humans could learn from. Little did I know of the effects this would have upon my life.

The first illustration of this came quickly. I was sitting in a Rotary meeting (I'm a new member and it was Max who had suggested I join this wonderful service organization) and the guy next to me was telling me about his daughter, who has a *therapy* dog.

That got my total attention! "What's a therapy dog?" I inquired, now focused on the man and his story.

"My daughter has a dog that she discovered is ultra sensitive to human feelings, especially those that kids with emotional disabilities have."

I sensed internally that this little conversation would open me up to a whole new understanding of life. You know what I mean by this. A new idea may at first seem so innocent, but then—wham!—it changes you to the core.

Totally captivated, I did the only thing that I could in this situation. I asked, "Could you have your daughter contact me? This is absolutely fascinating."

He did and she did, and soon we had a meeting at a local Starbucks where I would meet Mandy (the daughter) and Chaco (the dog) to hear their story.

After the normal chit-chat, Mandy got down to business by sharing her greatest life challenge—illness. Now thirty-six years old, at the way-to-early-age of twenty one, she suddenly developed "neuropathy," a disease of the nerves that results in great, great pain in the form of electric-like shocks throughout the body. Despite vast testing, no cause could be determined, leaving her with little hope of recovery. Following two years of feeling sorry for herself and lying around the house doing nothing, she finally realized that she had a decision to make: either get up and about, or waste away. She chose life.

Her family had always had Australian shepherds as pets. True to form, their newest dog was an Aussie and had recently been adopted to be her dad's dog. But Chaco had other ideas, mainly that he would be Mandy's dog and not her father's. They became best buddies and were together constantly.

However, when Chaco was around six years old, he did something incredible. Mandy had gone to her car one afternoon to run an errand and was becoming irritated with Chaco, who kept trying to prevent her from getting into the car and driving.

First he tried blocking her way. Then he stood up on his back legs with his paws on her shoulders. When she still wouldn't listen to him, he did the only thing possible: he lightly grabbed her hand with his mouth—the one holding the car keys.

That's when the seizure started. Mandy fell to the ground. When she came to, Chaco was lying across her body, licking her face.

After recovering, Mandy realized something quite extraordinary had happened—Chaco had sensed her seizure *before* she had felt the physical symptoms. It was this startling discovery that catapulted both of them onto a new life journey.

Mandy next began testing Chaco to see if this was just a rare occurrence or if he really had the ability to sense things in people even before they might be aware of it. She eventually discovered that Chaco's sensitivity to human emotions went way beyond that first incident and that he was a gifted animal.

To utilize those talents, Mandy and Chaco began doing volunteer work at Excelsior Youth Center and the Mental Health Center of Denver, Colorado. Working with deeply disturbed youngsters, she discovered that many had life journeys involving the horrors of rape, incest and most any of the other atrocious things the human mind can conjure up.

She discovered that where many of these young girls were unable to express the nightmares they had gone through, Chaco's presence—this sympathic, empathic and understanding dog they could reach out and touch—enabled them to begin voicing their dire experiences.

During one group session, one of the girls who had not shared her story finally spoke up. Sobbing, she said, "I've want to tell someone, but it is so painful to remember." Upon hearing the girl's distress and pain, Chaco, who had been sitting next to the girl but facing the center of the circle, did a one hundred eighty-degree turn, placed his paws on the girl's shoulders and began licking away her tears.

I've got to insert here that I was totally blown away by this dog. You would have been too if you had been there at that Starbucks that day.

As Mandy and I wrapped up our conversation, I looked under the table where Chaco was lying on the patio. He immediately stood up and began eyeing a slice of lemon cake I had in front of me. Mandy gently scolded him and informed me that she never fed Chaco from the table. As I stared into Chaco's beautiful, warm, loving blue eyes, I could almost swear he was using his ESP talents in communicating to me to not believe what Mandy had just said about the "not feeding from the table" thing. I was secretly pleased that this gifted animal was still all dog.

It was hard taking my eyes away from Chaco's haunting, accepting eyes. His eyes were so ethereal that a novel idea crossed my mind: *Could he be an angel in disguise?* And then my mind made another leap and asked, *were both Mandy and Chaco angels in disguise?*

After our parting, I confess that my heart was bursting with joy. Humbly awed, the world suddenly felt like a better place, and a small smile lingered on my lips for some time that day.

Chaco's official title is an *animal-assisted therapy dog*. He and Mandy went through rigorous training and assessment to ensure they both had the skills and aptitude to work safely and effectively as a team before ever starting to do volunteer work in this very complex mental health field. They work as a registered team as part of a non-profit organization called American Humane Association.

And believe it or not, Chaco receives many letters form the kids. One letter in particular really tugged at my heart. It said, "Chaco, thank you for loving me and never telling my secrets."

Do you see what I mean? Max and I had no more than made our decision to begin researching what animals were capable of when we were thrust into this fascinating story. I mean, this dog actually contributes to people's healing.

I began wondering what the next lesson would be.

Why does it seem
that our best friends so
often have four paws?

—Maxwell Winston Stone

Horses are like 1,000 pound mirrors. They reflect back to us exactly how we are feeling on the inside.

—Suzanne Carter, M.A., LPC

INTUITION IS THE ABILITY TO KNOW something, to attain direct knowledge of something without using verbal communication. Horses are proving to be the epitome of an intuitive being.

Older people enjoy reflecting back on their life. I knew Max liked to share and tell stories about his youth, so whenever he got in the mood to do so, I enjoyed hearing them as he was one of the best storytellers anywhere. Today he remembered his cowboy days when he worked on a dude ranch in Pinedale, Wyoming.

Max always began a path down memory lane with the preface, "Ernie, I remember when...," then his eyes would get that far-off look and I knew I was in for a treat.

"I remember when I was only fifteen years old when I finally ran away from home for good. It was a bad, bad place to grow up," his eyes darkened by his remembrances. I recalled the first time Max had explained where his name came from. "Maxwell Winston Stone," he said, "*Maxwell* for all the coffee my folks drank; *Winston* for all the cigarettes they smoked; and *Stone* (here was where the temperature in the room dropped a few degrees as Max's demeanor became darker)...I guess that represented their hearts."

He continued with his story. "The first place I stopped was in this little town of Pinedale, Wyoming and was lucky enough to nab a job on a dude ranch; I think it was called The Flying A Ranch. I started off doing all of the most distasteful jobs, though I didn't mind as long as I got room and board. Of course, I lied about my age, told them I was eighteen and had always looked young for my age.

"After I proved I was a good worker, they began letting me ride the horses. Later on, I rode in a real cattle roundup and ended up flipping the calves to be *fixed* and even branding a few.

"Now, I had never been around horses much so at first I was a bit hesitant around these huge creatures. But, eventually I struck up a friendship with the horse I had been riding named *Brownstone*." Max paused for a moment remembering. "I began to think that this horse was the smartest animal around. I mean it seemed to know how I was feeling inside and what I needed from him. Sometimes it was downright eerie."

***

I was recalling this story from Max when I overheard a conversation some people were having about horses being used by a psychotherapist in healing her clients. I immediately contacted Suzanne Carter, the horse psychotherapist they were talking about, explained about my book and we set up an interview.

Beautiful and bubbling with excitement she began by telling me that besides being a traditional psychotherapist, she was also an Equine Assisted Psychotherapist, an emerging new field, and began explaining this new technique. "Horses are great therapists because they are so honest and intuitive and reflect back to us our innermost feelings. For example," she said, "if a client is fearful inside and yet honestly shows this fear in their external actions, the horse is cool with this. But, if the client is nervous on the inside and attempts to hide it in their outside actions, the horse will never buy it and will be skittish."

She cited this example:

"During a first session with a new client, I asked her to put the halter on the horse...Now this was a person who had an eating disorder and was nervous being with the horse. The horse, sensing the discordance between her genuine inner feelings and the way she was acting, balked and would not allow her to position the halter.

"In the next session, I first worked with her to help alleviate her nervousness by some deep breathing exercises and centering down (which is a marvelous way to embrace our feelings). When she approached the horse this time, the halter slipped on easily.

"The third session proved even more informative. While the client was trying to lead the horse on the halter, the horse kept dropping its head down to eat the grass. The client, without any conscious connection with her own eating problems blurted out, 'You don't need to eat,'" and then immediately saw this connection between what she had just said to the horse and her own personal inner thinking about food. It was a real turning point in her therapy.

"See, oftentimes these horses give us immediate results—they help us to move from our minds to our hearts. They are simply great teachers and may be the most intuitive animals on our planet," she added.

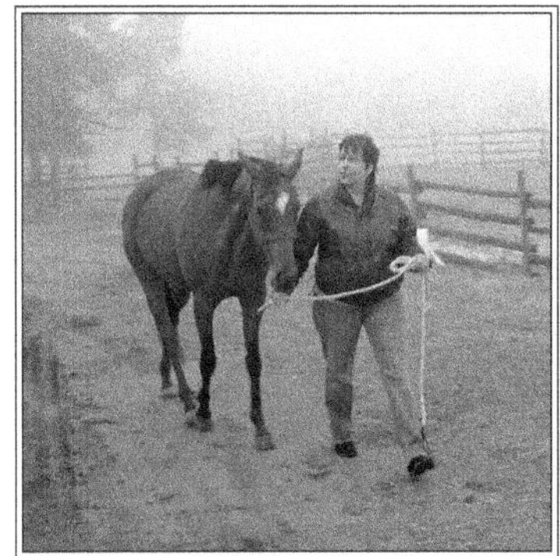

When I shared with Suzanne that I had recently been around some therapy dogs, her reply intrigued me. "Dogs also make wonderful therapy animals. However, the big difference between a horse and canine is that a dog is a people pleaser, meaning that it will adapt to the humans needs. Horses, on the other hand, are not people pleasers, and rely less upon their vision and more on external hearing and an inner knowing. A horse's behavior is almost always in alignment with how they feel about their own safety."

Our conversation flowed with Suzanne asking some rather thought-provoking questions:

"Why do some people say they find their souls while looking in the eyes of a horse?"

"Why do you think that horses, much stronger and powerful than we are, allow us to ride them and endure our sometimes even violent moods? Could they have been sent here to be our teachers?"

"How do we sense that horses know what we are feeling?"

She also made an interesting side comment to me. "Actually, my job is to simply ask the right question and then let the people project onto the horse what they are feeling. The horse then becomes the therapist."

Suzanne Carter is also an Associate Minister at the Unity Church of Denver. Another thing of interest that she along with others instituted at this remarkable church involves stuffed animals. If you ever visit the Unity Church of Denver, you will notice stuffed animals placed throughout the seats. It is interesting to watch newcomer's responses to them. At first, they are generally wary of the unreal animals. But then, during some point in the service and depending upon their emotional needs at the time, you see them reaching out and grasping tight to these little stuffed animals.

After interviewing Suzanne, I will never again approach a horse without intentionally identifying what I am feeling. I mean, seeing myself through a thousand pound mirror is quite a gift from these innately talented teachers.

A quote by psychotherapist Carl Jung appeared in my mind, "Those who go outside dream; those who go inside awaken."

If a man aspires toward a righteous life, his first act of abstinence is from injury to animals.

—ALBERT EINSTEIN
THEORETICAL PHYSICIST
(1879–1955)

FORMATION FLYING

IT WAS A BEAUTIFUL FALL DAY. Max and I were hiking in the Colorado mountains, something we did as often as I could get away. The sky was cobalt blue. The aspen trees shimmered in golden shades of yellow.

Looking up, Max pointed to a flock of geese flying in formation. We've all seen them numerous times and they are stunning. For many people, they evoke a yearning, a reminder that seasons change—that everything in the world changes.

But as the title of this book boldly states, most animals are highly intelligent and we can learn from these living things. Max began pointing out the lessons we can learn from geese.

"Ernie, did you know that a flock of geese can fly over seventy percent farther than a single goose alone?"

"What?" I looked at him rather incredulously.

"You bet," Max grandly pronounced. "They can because traveling as a flock conserves their energy. You see, each bird flies just above the bird in back of him, thus reducing the wind resistance and enabling it to expend less energy." And then he further stunned me by saying, "Just think of how much further we could go if we utilized this principle of all of us working together as *a planet*."

Where did Max come up with this incredible insight?

"Yep, and these birds naturally share responsibility by taking turns being the leader. When the lead goose (who is exerting the most energy because it experiences the greatest wind resistance) gets tired, it simply drops back into formation while another bird takes its place. This way the flock can fly farther without having to stop and rest. Plus, it just makes sense to take turns doing the hardest work.

"Now think about this, Ernie, wouldn't our world benefit by sharing leadership? Could this be used as an argument for limiting the terms of our elected officials and decreasing the possibilities that an ego-centered power base ever being established?"

I shook my head in amazement.

"See how they fly in a V formation?" he continued.

"It enables the group to more easily keep track of each member and allows more effective communication."

What a fantastic concept, I thought, *better care and concern for each other along with better communication.*

Max wasn't through yet. "Did you know that scientists believe that the honking we hear from the flying geese comes from the other geese behind the leaders encouraging them to keep up their speed?"

This lesson is easy: how much better could our world be if we encouraged each other rather than criticized?

Max concluded with this last insight: "When a goose is shot or becomes ill, two other geese will drop out of the formation, follow the ill goose down to earth and stay with it until it either dies or gets better. Then they all will join up with another flock until they catch up with their own."

Wow! You talk about loving and supporting one another. We could certainly use much more of this.

Max ended these lessons with this statement. "We are all surrounded by such magnificent mysteries—if we only took the time to learn from our animal friends, our world would be a much better place."

"Amen," was all I could say.

Apprehend God in all things, for God is in all things. Every single creature is full of God and is a book about God. Every creature is a word of God.

—Meister Eckhart
Thirteenth Century Mystic

THIS ANIMAL SPOKE TO THE WORLD

The year was 1972, and psychology graduate student Penny Patterson began work on her Ph.D. project at Stanford University in Northern California. She chose to work with a fragile young gorilla named Hanabi-Ko at the San Francisco zoo. Little did she realize at the time but that one decision would reverberate around the world and alter the course her life journey would take. I recalled the words of the poet Robert Frost, "Two paths diverged in the woods, and I, I took the one less traveled by."

Why? What happened?

The soon-to-be Dr. Patterson made the startling discovery that this gorilla, nicknamed Koko, had the ability to actually communicate using signs she had been taught and demonstrated an understanding of English words. It seemed Koko had something to say. In fact, she had much to say (and share) with Dr. Patterson, and with the rest of the world.

Within the first two weeks, she watched Koko babble with her hands at bedtime, and use the correct signed gestures for *food* and *drink*. And within the first year, Koko began to sign to herself, use new word combinations, ask questions and comment about her environment.

"Project Koko" was born.

The thing that surprised Dr. Patterson and her colleagues the most was the speed with which Koko learned sign language. What scientists eventually came to understand, through close observation of zoo gorillas, was that gorillas communicate naturally among themselves with gestures. Koko's learning curve was so fast because the gorilla brain is *wired* for signing, just like humans.

Thirty plus years later, Koko had become the most well-known gorilla in the world. She had developed a signing vocabulary of more than one-thousand signed words and an understanding of over two-thousand spoken words.

Thus, one of the greatest animal stories of all times revealed itself: a gorilla who could communicate with our species. And a beautiful love story unfolded. It

would disprove the stereotyped image of gorillas being seen as ogres and frightening monsters. It would forever change the way that humans viewed animals.

Koko, a female lowland gorilla born in 1971, disclosed to the world that animals do possess imagination and feelings, creativity and complicated thought processes. Communicating with Koko has given animal advocates powerful new information for the prevention of cruelty to animals and the protection of endangered species.

As for the love story, this too would emerge.

***

"Hey, Max, do you remember a long time ago about a gorilla named Koko?"

Max began nodding his head in recognition.

"Well, I just got off the telephone with a representative of the Gorilla Foundation who authorized me to include the story in the book."

"That will be a good addition, Ernie. But do you know what I remember most about Koko?"

"What?" I asked.

"Koko's relationship with a little cat named, I think, All Ball. Seeing this huge and fierce looking gorilla nurture and take care of this tiny little furry creature was so heartwarming. I remember it as a love affair that melted people's hearts everywhere. They wrote a book specifically about their relationship. It's titled, ***KOKO'S KITTEN***.

"I remember that, but didn't the kitten die somehow?" I recalled.

"Yes, but to see the picture of Koko holding and loving All Ball, it strongly reinforced the novel idea that she was just as much of a person as you and I. I remember reading that Koko's greatest desire was to have a baby. "Can you believe that?" Max said. "She was able to communicate this beautiful desire through sign language with Dr. Patterson.

"What began as an initial four-year project would evolve into a life long destiny for Dr. Patterson. It certainly radically changed the way we humans would forever perceive animals," I added.

"Imagine a huge gorilla loving a tiny cat. That brings me hope for our world."

Max was nodding emphatically yes.

Animals are such agreeable friends. They ask no questions; they pass no criticisms.

—George Eliot
English Novelist
(1819–1880)

THE CITY DOG AND THE COUNTRY DOG

"Max, I've got a story for you."

Max's face lit up. Even though he was the storyteller, he also loved to hear stories from others.

"I had a friend once who was a great guy. He was also one of the most insecure people I knew. Now, there was nothing for him to be insecure about, he just was. During college he fell head over heels for a woman who was beautiful. After pleading with her again and again to marry him, she finally agreed and my friend was simply ecstatic."

"Their marriage went well for a while. He was loving and supportive to her and her to him, until his insecurities reared their ugly heads, causing him to become jealous and possessive. He became so afraid of losing her that he constantly tried to prevent her from doing anything *without* him; he would raise a stink whenever she went out with girlfriends, or even to visit her parents without him.

"This continued until finally, and you've probably already guessed it, his wife did the thing he feared the most—she left him. She told him that with him she always felt she was in a prison, restricted from doing the normal things she felt were necessary for her life.

"I lost touch with him somewhere along the way, but thought about him when I heard the story of 'The Country Dog and the City Dog.'"

> Once upon a time, there was a city dog. Now this city dog was raised in an apartment and never let free to roam. The only time he ever left the apartment was for walks, and even then he had to be muzzled and led on a leash. He constantly yearned to be free and took off any chance he got.
>
> At the same time, there was also a dog that lived in the country. Like all country dogs he was left free to roam the countryside, chase wild animals and bark and bite at car tires when it approached its house...Now the interesting thing was

> that although this dog could go anywhere it wanted at any time, do you know where it stayed most of the time?
>
> You got it, on the porch, free to leave any time it wished.

"I learned an interesting paradox from this country/city dog story, Max, that I hope I have conveyed to my wife: *try to imprison someone, and they will want to run away—give them freedom, and they may want to stay.*"

Max's appreciative facial expression warmed my heart. Then he added to the story with this: "Do you remember that painting from a while ago? It pictured a hand opening to let the butterfly soar away. The caption on the picture read, 'Only when you release someone into freedom, is there a chance they will return on their own free will.'"

Life is like a dogsled team.
If you ain't the lead dog,
the scenery never changes.

—Lewis Grizzard
American Humorist and Writer

A MOST AMAZING BIRD

AVE YOU EVER HEARD OF A "lyrebird?"

Only found on the continent of Australia, these birds are best known for their incredible ability to mimic both natural and artificial sounds in their environment.

I first heard about this bird's extraordinary ability to mimic *any* sound it hears while watching a television show. Imagine my amazement in hearing one of these species reproduce the sounds of such surprising things as human noises, all kinds of different machinery, even a chainsaw, a baby crying, a rifle shot, car engines, or car alarms. After only hearing any noise once, the lyrebird reproduces that sound perfectly. They seem to have a photographic memory for sounds as some humans have photographic memories of everything they read.

There is a story about a male lyrebird named James who formed a close relationship with a human being named Mrs. Wilkinson. Because she had been feeding him, James would perform his courtship dance for her on a mound he had constructed in her backyard. Later on, he even began doing his fascinating-to-watch performance with others present as long as Mrs. Wilkinson was present.

One of James's dances actually lasted forty-three minutes, and included his perfect mimicry of the sounds he had heard earlier of a rock-crusher, a hydraulic ram and the beeping from automobiles.

Or try this: Imagine that you are with a hiking party in Australia in a quite remote area. There are no cars or roads or houses, just wilderness. Yet, you suddenly hear the roar of a lawnmower—the sound so real that you redirect your course to try and find the location of the mower. After much searching, you finally come upon a strange looking bird with its tail all fanned out and you realize the sound was coming from it—a sound exactly like a lawn mower!

You might Google "lyrebird" and hear for yourself some of the mind-blowing mimicry this bird is capable of.

There is no psychiatrist in the world like a puppy licking your face.

—Ben Williams

OPERATION RESCUE

"ERNIE, HOW DO YOU FEEL ABOUT this photo of the young horse nearly starved to death?"

"Sick to my stomach, Max."

"The photo shows how the horse looked upon arriving at *Colorado Horse Rescue*. I heard the story began when County Sheriff's Department seized over two hundred abused and neglected mustangs on animal

abuse and neglect charges; they found dozens of dead foals and starving, mature horses in the pasture, along with a pony they named Little Boodah."

Max continued, "Extremely small for his age and with a coat four times as thick and long as normal; he had little flesh on his bones. You see, so little meat caused his body to produce more hair in attempt to stay warm. Also, his belly was quite distended because of all the parasites in his stomach. All of these things combined to make it clear that he would never be big enough to carry a human. Thus, there would be great difficulty in placing him with a family.

"But then, a small miracle took place. Colorado Horse Rescue's barn manager made the decision that Little Boodah would come to the ranch. Her reasoning? 'Because I wanted to give the cute little guy a chance.'

"Here's what's neat, Ernie. Because Little Boodah had never learned to be afraid of humans and still had the capacity to trust, his learning curve was spectacular. But the biggest change of all came from inside the horse in the form of *attitude*—from a meek, sickly, stunted yearling, he evolved into a confident, outgoing, too-big-for-his-shoes mustang. It was uplifting to witness. And like all happy stories, they soon placed him with a horsewoman who fell deeply in love with him and who had a duo of mares on her ranch that treat him like their own."

Now see how Boodah looked after much love and caring.

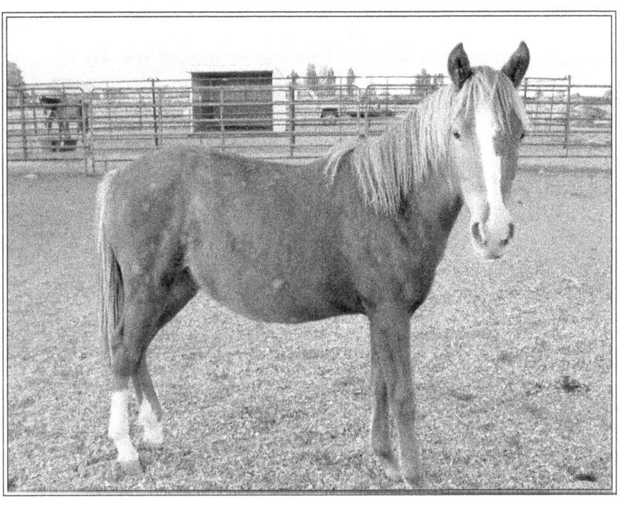

This little horse represents the power of *determination*. All he needed was a little help, a break in life that allowed his fierce desire to live to inspire every human who had contact with him.

***

"You know, Ernie, buying a horse has been compared to buying a hot tub. At first, you are excited over your new purchase and use it every day. But then, after a year or so, after the novelty has worn off, you find yourself spending less and less time with your now *old* purchase. However, the difference between these two items is huge. Where the hot tub is an inanimate object, a horse is a living, breathing creature with which you have entered into a relationship. You are the human and *are* responsible to this animal. It depends upon you."

I nodded in agreement.

"Unfortunately, way too many horses are slaughtered simply because people no longer want them. Many people have begun questioning this act by asking the uncomfortable statement, 'If we kill our horses because they no longer seem to be of use, is this only a short step away from us doing the same thing to humans?' "

The greatness of a nation and its moral progress can be judged by the way its animals are treated.

—Mahatma Gandhi

Spiritual leader who first used nonviolent civil disobedience

(1869–1948)

Who's helping who?

It begins here: two broken souls reaching out and searching for trust, love and compassion.

—Jodi and Paul Messenich
Owners, Zuma's Rescue Ranch

Did you know **that about 130,000 horses are slaughtered for meat every year?**

How about that there are 1.3 million children who are either homeless or in foster care?

What about this one: eighty percent of inmates in our prisons were once in foster care?

Now, with these three facts in mind, the optimum question might be wouldn't it be creative if somehow these horses destined to be killed could be paired with the foster kids and that this new relationship would save and heal both of them?

Guess what? Because of such people like Jodi and Paul Messenich and their *Zuma's Rescue Ranch,* this miracle is taking place *right now.*

Max rode along with me on the drive out to the Zuma Rescue Ranch. We were excited to see what new discoveries we would make this time. After introductions were made, Jodi began, "Our mission is to simply save horses, rehabilitate them and then *pair* them with emotionally broken children who are overrunning our society. Together they can learn from one another to love and trust in a world that has failed them in some way."

Then Paul interjected, "By pairing the community's troubled kids with these once cast-off horses, we create a unique opportunity to heal them both.

"Equine Assisted Experiential Learning is a way of *treating* the animals and kids together and ends up with a much higher success rate than with traditional therapy," he says. "See, it's through the horse's body language that the children learn to get in touch with their own feelings and begin to trust the most basic of human emotions—instinct."

Jodi added, "It is all about bonding, and in any bonding, what happens is that a close relationship develops, and nothing is more obvious than the bonding that takes place between a human and an animal."

***

I immediately recalled a story told to me by an author friend of mine, Bill Hubiak. He said that he had a dog named

Ferbie, who totally loved and trusted him. He had been traveling a lot and discovered upon his return that his dog would not deliver her litter of puppies until he was home and he actually could help with the delivery.

"As soon as I walked in the front door, Ernie, Ferbie looked at me and then at her back end as if to say, 'Cup your hands and catch each of my pups.' Then she let loose and the babies came. After cleaning up her pups, as exhausted as she must have been (she had a litter of twelve puppies), she still came to rest her head in my lap and lick my hands. This is the type of bond we had established," he said with tears in his eyes.

I then remembered some facts Max had shared with me. "Originally, Ernie, animals were categorized almost exclusively in a functional role, e.g., sheep dogs herding sheep, cats killing mice. Today in the West it is a whole new ballgame. Did you know that sixty to eighty percent of dogs sleep in the same bedroom with their owners, either on the bed or the floor? That most cats, once assigned only to the barn, now sleep in the house and are considered a part of the family? Or, that there are over 1.2 billion pets in the worlds that are kept for the primary purpose of bonding with humans?"

***

The Messenich's Zuma Rescue Ranch currently has thirty-nine horses and takes in as many troubled kids as they can possibly handle with a limited budget. The only thing limiting them is *money*.

"We don't exactly know how these rescued horses bond with the kids," Paul said. "What we do know is that somehow these horses enhance a child's self-esteem, teach them responsibility and those that have been a part of this program later become more involved in sports, hobbies, clubs, and even chores.

"One of the boy's had been caught up in the system and sent to a new foster family on a regular basis. He was angry and had never experienced anything about how a healthy relationship is supposed to work. No one seemed to want him, except the horse, who taught him about such vital personal understandings as acceptance, responsibility and love, traits he had never seen exhibited before.

"And the horses...they too get healed," Paul added. "It seems the benefits of this bonding go both ways."

***

"Max, can you see this picture? Look at the expression in the boy's face. Is that bonding, or what?"

This is what you should do; love the Earth and the sun and the animals.

—Walt Whitman
American poet
(1819–1892)

THE LONG JOURNEY HOME

MAX AND I were focusing much of our days on discovering the ways that animals were healing us. He called one morning quite excited over what he had recently found on the internet.

"Ernie, I just read about the cat that made its way from the East Coast to California, a distance of almost 3, 000 miles."

"What!" I mumbled.

"This is one for the books, Ernie…the story goes that the father of the family had lost his job and was desperate to find a new one. After putting out a ton of job applications, he finally received a job offer in California. The job was a good one and would require the family moving from New York City, the place where their families had lived for many generations.

"After packing up all their household possessions in a van to set out on their journey, they carried the family cat, their most prized family pet to the truck to begin the long drive across country. However, the cat seemed to have other plans as it jumped out of their arms and ran away. As the story goes, they searched and searched but had no luck finding it. After much fretting they made the soul-wrenching decision to leave the poor thing to survive on its own.

"Now, here's where all logic and reasoning goes out the door. Two months after getting settled in California, one of the kids heard a cat mewing at the front door. Opening it, they found *their cat* on their front doorstep! Though looking ragged, disheveled and quite thin, this little animal none-the-less had found his way back to its family and began meowing and rubbing up against every family member's legs.

"You see the deep emotional attachment between humans and the animal kingdom that was so vividly portrayed here," Max concluded with eyes filled with tears.

"You've got to be kidding me, Max. How did the cat get there?"

His voice filled with wonder, Max whispered into the phone, "They never figured it out..."

A SIXTH SENSE

MAX AND I often had great discussions together. Like the time I asked him if an animal can sense when a person is going to die.

"Of course not, only God knows when a person is going to die," my friend replied.

"Then you are going to love this one. Believe it or not, it does seem that some animals have this very rare ability—specifically a cat named Oscar who lives in a nursing home in Rhode Island. After five years of recording this feline's talent, he has proven to be more reliable than the doctors and nurses at predicting more *thirty deaths*.

"Interestingly, the cat is normally not very sociable and spends little time with any of the patients, until, *yes he does,* he curls up next to a patient who has on the average less than two hours to live."

"Come on, Ernie, that one sounds like a whopper to me," he insisted.

"Nope, it's apparently documented by doctors associated with the nursing home."

"This is something," Max said, shaking his head in wonder. "I guess it must be like dogs that can smell cancer."

"Say what?" I said, startled by this new bit of information.

"Yep," there are dogs that can do this also," Max said.

My mind began whirling. "How about the dogs that can sniff out bombs or those that smell drugs?"

"Or those that can tell when an insulin attack is imminent?" Max threw in.

"Why haven't we relied more upon these creatures?" Max's voice conveyed sadness. "Why haven't we given them more respect? What other talents do animals have that we are not yet aware of?"

We sat in silence, pondering these ever increasingly significant questions.

Do you want to try an experiment on who loves you the most—your dog or your wife/husband? Put both of them in the trunk of your car on a very hot day for an hour. Then open the trunk and see which one is happy to see you.

—Anonymous

WHEN IS A DUCK A GOOSE?

I WAS STANDING IN A LINE at a store when a man and I began talking. As the conversation eventually turned in the direction of what I did for a living, I said that I was an author and working on my eighth book in a series and this book was about animals, specifically about traits that animals exhibit from which we humans could learn.

At that point the man's whole demeanor lit up and he said, "Boy, do I have a story for you. I had a well-trained bird dog, a flat-coated retriever," he said. "I mean this was the greatest bird dog I have ever had or had ever seen before. This dog did things that were beyond belief!"

"Like what?" I asked, beginning to share in his enthusiasm.

"One time we were out hunting ducks. When two flew over, I shot one of them and it fell in the water.

Looking down at my quivering-with-excitement-dog, I told him to go fetch and I marked the area where I saw the bird had gone down.

"After a couple of minutes the dog returned *without* the duck, a failure I had not experienced with him before. So I pointed out the directional line of where I had marked the downed bird and told him again to go fetch.

"Five minutes later he returned, again with no bird. I was getting not only frustrated but also a bit shocked that this incredible dog of mine had failed a second time. So, I pointed out the directional line and for the third time told him to *go fetch*.

"So I waited, and waited, and waited. After what seemed ten or fifteen minutes the dog finally returned this time with a bird in his mouth…only it wasn't a duck, it was a goose!" the man exploded with laughter.

"A goose," I said, somewhat astonished, "But how?"

Still laughing the man said, "You know I never figured it out. All I know is that dog really wanted to please me and would just not give up until he returned with some kind of bird. That's why I said he was the most tenacious dog I've ever seen."

Dogs are miracles
with paws.

—Attributed to
Susan Ariel Rainbow Kennedy

"HE DOESN'T EVEN KNOW HE'S DISABLED!"

"MAX, REMEMBER THE interview I had with Mandy and her therapy dog Chaco?"

"How could I forget it? Chaco's eyes were so mysterious."

"Well, before leaving the interview, Mandy suggested I contact a friend of hers who also has a therapy dog that was born in a puppy mill and had only two legs. Unfortunately, both legs were on the right side. This makes walking and running rather precarious."

I had done some research on puppy mills before our meeting.

"If you don't know what a *puppy mill* is, let me enlighten you. Primarily, it is a *commercial* breeding facility that is operated for profit and with little emphasis on the well-being of the dogs in their care. Females are often bred every time they go into heat to ensure the highest profits, but this eventually begins decreasing the size of their litters. The puppies are usually weaned (taken from their mothers) way before the recommended eight to ten weeks. Because of the vastly crowded conditions, most of the dogs become poorly socialized to both other dogs and humans. Puppy mill dogs are more prone to developing respiratory ailments, pneumonia and an array of heredity defects. Oprah Winfrey, on MSNBC in May of 2008, revealed puppy mills had cages way too small for the animals, chicken wire floors (that can trap dogs' paws and legs) and cages that were stacked in rows from floor to ceiling. She said that many of these dogs spend their entire brief lives in these tiny cramped cages."

Max was shaking his head in disgust.

"This is where the little two-legged, Sheltie dog pictured on previous page came from. His name, *Dare,* is short for Dare To Find the Truth About Puppy Mills. Originally born with all four legs, one leg was most likely gnawed off by his mother. You see, many of the dogs go *cage crazy* in the cramped conditions, and the poor mother probably didn't know what she was even doing. The other leg had been caught in the cage wiring and broken in so many places it proved beyond repair. It had to be amputated by a veterinarian when Dare was given to animal rescue."

I know that there are great tragedies that occur in the human condition also, but I wondered how many of us humans could continue on after such a dire beginning.

"When I asked Dare's owner, Tami, why she decided to keep a two-legged dog and agree to all the extra work it would entail, she first looked at me like I was nuts, then explained, 'Because the first time I saw him I just knew that I was just somehow tied to him and he to me…that somehow I sensed that Dare had a higher purpose for being here on earth…plus,' she smiled big, 'he has quite an attitude. He never quits!'"

"The higher purpose soon revealed itself. Dare and Tami do volunteer work at hospitals where Dare inspires human amputees. Tami says that she has heard many times from amputees, "When I see this dog who is missing two legs, it makes me realize that my one amputation is not so significant. I mean if he can do it, so can I."

They also spend time at a school for kids with severe physical disabilities. "Dare provides those kids with acceptance," Tami said, "where other kids might say, 'I like you but…' (meaning they don't like the kid's disability nor drooling), Dare simply doesn't look at them as different. Dare simply gives them acceptance as they are; acceptance with no conditions...and don't forget, they accept Dare right back."

"But my most memorable experience," she began, "was a thirty-year-old man who needed to have his foot amputated in order to live but kept cancelling appointments. One evening, he finally showed up and immediately gravitated to Dare. When it was time for the group meeting, he asked if Dare was going and when told yes, shocked everyone by deciding to attend.

"During that first meeting," Tami explained, her face aglow, "I was surprised even more when the man spoke up during the meeting and talked about his fears about going through with the amputation all the while holding and stroking Dare. He concluded by saying, 'If Dare could handle it, so can I.' "

Tami also shared this charming little story. "When Dare plays with his four other Sheltie brothers, they all play well together. But what is so amazing is that when Dare becomes tired sooner than the other dogs because of his only two leg situation, one of the other dogs will allow Dare to lean on him—will stand perfectly still—until Dare recovers."

"Dare, like Chaco, is an *animal-assisted therapy dog.* He and Tami went through rigorous training classes to earn this title and work as a registered team as part of a nonprofit organization called *American Humane*, just like Chaco and Mandy."

"People so often tell me that Dare is so lucky to have *me*," Tami quietly said, "but the real truth is that *I* am the lucky one. He has enriched my life beyond words."

"Dare inspires me daily," she added. "You know, when a human is injured, they focus on the damaged area, the negative, and feel sorry for themselves. But an animal doesn't—they accept it, adapt and move on with life. Dare has the most phenomenal attitude... Why, he doesn't even know he's disabled."

Of course, Max had tears in his eyes and couldn't speak, certainly a rare situation for this storyteller.

***

Self-Pity

I never saw a wild
thing sorry for itself.

A small bird will drop frozen
dead from a bough, without ever
having felt sorry for itself.

—D.H. LAWRENCE

Lots of people talk to animals...Not very many listen, though... that's the problem.

—Benjamin Hoff,
American Author *The Tao of Pooh*

Joyce Leake, Animal Whisperer

Photograph by Sherry Slade, Parker, Colorado

I WAS SO ENGROSSED finishing up reading a book that I didn't hear Max walk in and jumped when he spoke.

"Holy smokes. You startled me," I exclaimed.

"That book you're reading must be some book," Max said. "What's it on?"

I smiled in response. "Max, it's written by an *animal whisperer,* someone who can not only communicate with animals, but also actually can hear them speak to her."

"I've heard of people like that," Max said nodding. "How in the world do they do it?"

Looking down at the book's front cover, my eyes scanned the book's title, ***DECODING THE MYSTERY OF INTERSPECIES COMMUNICATION*** by Joyce Leake and Vickie Wickhorst, I gathered my thoughts.

"Basically, they are saying that we humans have many more capabilities than we were ever aware of and that being able to communicate with other animals is just one of those abilities. They firmly believe that all humans have the capacity to both talk and hear animals speaking."

"Wow!" Max whispered, "But how?"

"Both of these women believe that *all* animals can communicate with each other (e.g. dogs with horses, horses to birds, and humans with other animals). That we are all linked together through a communication channel, a mode of communication that is quite subtle, though very real.

"Furthermore, they propose that intuitive communication, or telepathy, isn't magic or voodoo, nor is it a special psychic gift meant for only a few. Just like our other senses, intuition is something we are born with. Unlike our other senses, it is less visible, less physical and therefore less trusted in the western world," I recalled. "Then, like intuition, it is a form of higher level communication."

"Ernie, this sounds fascinating," Max stated, shaking his head in wonderment.

"Astonishingly, Max, they write that we have always possessed the ability to hear our dog or cat, but the simple reason of not using it caused us to forget we have the ability. But this is what blew me away, they assure us that with attention and practice we will open up new ways of thinking; that our brain will actually learn to process information in new and interesting ways.

"In fact, Max, Joyce is so certain we all can learn to be animal whisperers that she started *ANIMAL UNIVERSITY* to teach people how to develop this intuitive ability; or, better said, to teach them to *remember* this ability."

"No kidding?" Max responded, quite impressed.

"Let me read some parts of the book that I underlined:

> Interspecies communication is less about animals than it is about you. It's about your willingness to be open to the possibility that you *can* communicate with another species...
>
> The key is to train your brain to pick up and process information in different channels.
>
> The challenge for us is to refine our ability to receive the communication.
>
> Interspecies communication offers the participant the opportunity to learn more

> about themselves than they originally bargained for. It is a life altering experience.
>
> Animals have been waiting their entire lives for you to hear them.
>
> The pathway to our *original self* is through rediscovering intuition.

Max was laughing now. "Once again, Ernie, these animals are teaching us something rather spectacular; that a whole new arena of inner talents and abilities exist for everyone. Do you think we will ever fully grasp these lessons?"

"That's the key, isn't it Max. Will we ever allow them to be our teachers in some of the mysteries of life?"

***

> When asked, "How can I learn to communicate with animals?" my response is: "You don't necessarily need to learn how; you may need to just remember that you can." Perhaps if you give yourself a little more time to reflect, you'll recall how on your own. I know that is how it worked for me and I was just as anxious to learn as you.
>
> —Joyce Leake

Wild animals seldom kill for sport, man is the only one to whom the torture and death of his fellow creatures is amusing in itself.

—JAMES A. FROUDE
HISTORIAN AND NOVELIST
(1879–1955)

LESSONS FROM A LADDER

Hi, I'm Mary Carwile, Ernie's wife.

We love our house. It isn't huge. It doesn't sit amid fifteen acres of meticulously manicured lawn, nor can we brag of a long, circular driveway. But what it does have is a spectacular location on a charming little duck pond in an overly abundant treed subdivision. For us, it is like living in the Garden of Eden. When we sit on our south-facing deck in the late afternoon, the flower smells and serenity are only enhanced by presence of ducks, squirrels, bunnies and birds.

And just off our bedroom, we have another prized area; a small atrium. Because of its secluded location, we are able to leave our double bedroom doors open throughout the nights, immensely enjoying the evening breezes and nocturnal sounds.

I love sleeping late on Sunday mornings, and my husband normally respects this little pleasure of mine; but not this one morning. Rolling over and peeking out of just one eye, I saw him carrying a ladder out into the atrium. "Whatever," I said and rolled back over and shut my eyes extra tight, hoping to slip back into dreamland. That's when I heard him speaking to me.

In a half whisper he said, "Mary, honey, a large squirrel awakened me chattering so loudly and in such a unique way that I got up and went out on the atrium. It was on my third trip out there that I finally saw a small squirrel hiding behind one of the flower pots. It must have fallen off the roof. I think if you help me we can get her free." Then he added most earnestly, "I think she's really scared."

Well, who could ignore that?

My husband loves animals...No, no, no, I mean he *really* loves them. He is forever stopping and talking to them, wherever we are. You see, he truly believes they have a soul, and anytime he sees one, any kind—dog, cat, bird, rabbit, squirrel, fish, caterpillar, snake, it doesn't matter what, he simply stops and talks to them. What is even more eerie is that some of the times, I believe they are aware of this and the animals try to communicate back to him in some fashion;

like the time he stopped to speak to a large fish in an aquarium. You wouldn't have believed how this fish responded.

My sleeping was obviously over, so I agreed and disengaged myself from the seductive and comfy covers and stumbled out of bed.

"I think this is what we should do," he explained, "You go stand near the one side of the flower pot. I'll hold this box on the other side. When she runs out from behind, I'll catch her, carry her out the front door, and then release her."

Is he crazy? I secretly thought, but said, "Sure, sweetie."

So, we tried his plan. I guess squirrels don't know the rules. She ran alright—right into the box and just as fast *back out*, then continued running until she made four laps around the atrium. All the while I was holding up my sleep shirt, hopping from one foot to the other and desperately hoping the damn squirrel wouldn't run up my leg.

When she finally slowed down enough to find her hiding spot behind the flower pot, my husband and I looked at each other, him trying to keep his laughter to a minimum over my antics. I vaguely remember him mentioning a Plan B.

Plan B turned out to be simpler, easier and a heck of a lot safer. It entailed my husband repositioning the ladder so that if the squirrel could figure it out, she could return to the roof.

We then returned to our bed where we could observe the proceedings, and what a comedy it turned out to be. The little squirrel finally garnered the courage to peek out and survey the situation. We became hopeful when we noticed she focused right on the small rug my husband had propped up from the atrium's floor to the first rung of the ladder. Nice, huh? The little animal wouldn't even have to work very hard to get out.

But did she get it? Oh, no. Not at all. We just couldn't believe how easy it looked for us but were amazed how the little squirrel couldn't see her options. And then that thought bridged an idea to our minds—*do we do that also? Are there ladders in our own lives that we just don't see? Do we struggle and blame and cry "poor me" when the solution is right there in front of us?*

Now, here is when something fantastic happened. Do you remember the other larger squirrel, the one that originally warned my husband of what happened to his buddy? Well, he appeared on the roofline and then cautiously crawled down the ladder from the roof.

Then, believe it or not, he began making trips up and down the ladder, trying to show the other one what to do. I swear he was saying, "Here. Just follow me."

We quietly lay in our bed watching the show for nearly forty minutes. Finally, after being shown over and over what to do, the little gal followed the larger one up the ladder, onto the roof and both ran off chattering all the way.

Was there a lesson here? What aren't we aware of in our own lives? Can two squirrels and a ladder bring us truth and light in the middle of a sleepy Sunday morning?

The idea for us both, beyond the obvious one of one animal coming to the aid of another, was, *what solutions are we not seeing that would solve the problem in which we so often find ourselves? I mean, what if our Creator is jumping up and down trying to show us an obvious solution that is right before our eyes?*

Maybe all we just need is a couple of little furry friends to show us the way.

An animal's eyes have
the power to speak a
great many languages.

—Martin Buber
Theologian
(1878–1965)

READING TO DOGS

AX."

"What?"

"I just read about another way that animals are helping humans," I said shaking my head in wonderment.

Smiling, Max said, "Tell me about it."

"Did you know that they have discovered that elementary students who read to therapy dogs have their reading abilities soar?"

Max's eyes bore into mine. "Huh?" he said.

"You heard me right. Educators have experimented with elementary students reading to these animals and found that the young student's reading abilities greatly improved."

Max smiled in amazement.

"It is so easy. The children read to the dogs. The dogs listen and don't laugh, or tease, or judge the young reader. They also discovered that the dogs love to be read to and proved to be non-judgmental, caring listeners."

"I heard someone say that the act of *real* listening is like a great opera house where every sound returns fuller and richer," Max interjected.

"Max, that's beautiful."

"Yep!" he replied with absolutely no humility at all.

Laughing, I continued. "What educators discovered was that children who read at a lower level than their peers were usually intimidated by reading aloud in a group, had lower self-esteem and saw reading as a chore.

"Furthermore, they found that these children would much rather read to an animal than another person. Why? Because they knew the animals would never point out their limitations and would be more accepting and much less intimidating."

"That's all that's involved in the students improving their reading skills?" Max asked.

"Yes. The younger children just read to the dog under the supervision of an older student. Research reveals that the young readers gain confidence in reading to the dogs.

"And this process also helps autistic kids' reading abilities, Max."

"I wonder if we humans could learn something about this gift of listening while not judging another person," Max added.

"Like what?"

"Well, like when the theologian Paul Tillich wrote, 'The first duty of love is to listen.'

"Remember, Ernie, the Creator gave us two ears and only one mouth. Maybe we could learn from our animal friends to listen more and speak less."

"Max, I like that."

> Deep listening is miraculous for both the listener and the speaker. When someone receives us with open-hearted, non-judging, intensely interested listening, *our spirits expand.*
>
> —Sue Patton Thoele, Author, Psychotherapist and Inspirationist

The following poem was written for humans by a human. However, these reading/listening dogs seem to have known this truth all along:

Listening

When I ask you to listen to me and you start giving me advice, you have not done what I asked.

When I ask you to listen to me and you begin telling me why I shouldn't feel that way, you are trampling on my feelings.

When I ask you to listen to me and you feel you have to try to solve my problem, you have failed me.

Listen! All I asked was that you listen, not talk or do—just hear me.

Perhaps that's why prayer works—God is always there LISTENING.

So, please listen and just hear me. And, if you want to talk, wait a minute for your turn and I'll listen to you.

If you have men who will exclude God's creatures from the shelter of compassion and pity, you will have men who will deal likewise with their fellow men.

—St. Francis of Assisi
Patron Saint of Animals
(1181–1226)

"A new idea has emerged—the idea that prisoners, perhaps the most shunned segment of our society, be paired up with unadoptable animals that were going to be destroyed. By putting these two elements together, a new synergy was created and our planet's consciousness rises."

"ERNIE, HAVE YOU HEARD ABOUT prisoner trained dogs?"

"A little bit, Max. What do you know about it?" *I knew that Max always loved to inform me of something I hadn't known before.*

Suppressing a small grin, Max began, "Well, first of all, let me begin by letting you know the results of the program. At the Washington State Prison, 100% of the inmates who participated in the program found jobs upon being released. And, after three years, they had a recidivism rate (percentage of former prisoners who were rearrested and returned to prison) of *ZERO*."

That got my attention.

"This was one of those rare situations where everyone won: the prisoners, society and the dogs."

"Go on, go on."

"First, the animals benefit because they get to live, and the training they receive makes them infinitely more valuable.

"Most of the dogs were going to be destroyed because they had become unadoptable. From the prisoners, however, they were taught such socialization skills as basic manners training, to sit, to greet a person, to sit before going through a door, training for both being in a crate as well as house training and how to act when on a leash. With these practical new skills, their value to a society grew immensely.

"Some of these dogs showed more capabilities and therefore had further training in understanding hand signals and agility equipment. A few especially gifted animals received advance training for seizure alerts, the disabled and helper/aides for people with multiple sclerosis and autism.

"Now the community benefits from not only not having to destroy hundreds of animals, but also because it now has well-trained pets that are in great demand. Each dog's training is estimated to have a value of upward of $10,000.

"And for the prisoners, they win in just about every conceivable way. They learn how to groom, train and board the animals, knowledge that will prove highly advantageous for them obtaining employment upon their release from prison, normally a huge stumbling block for newly released prisoners.

"But more importantly, the prisoners learn such vital things like *joy, compassion, patience and responsibilities* that could not be learned in any classroom—that could only come from raising and training a dog."

I could tell Max was hiding something from me, but I waited until he was ready to share. Finally, you could tell when he just couldn't keep the new information inside himself any longer he finally spewed out, "How would you like to interview a guy who had been sentenced to a twenty-year stretch in a maximum security prison and was in the Prison Trained Dog Program?"

"Is he still in jail?" I asked, a bit taken aback.

"Oh no, he's been out since 2008 and is still working with dogs."

"What's his name? When is the interview?" I could feel my excitement growing.

Max could too. "His name is Joe, and here's his number so you can set up an appointment."

I called Joe on the way home from Max's and he suggested we meet on Saturday morning at a Denny's restaurant.

THE INTERVIEW

First of all, Joe turned out to be delightful. Both open and open-minded, his honesty and sincerity were obvious; his story captivating.

He readily explained that he had been given a twenty year prison term for "cooking" meth for resale. After serving about two years of his sentence, he underwent extensive interviewing to be included in the dog training. As this was quite an elite opportunity, few prisoners were accepted into the program. Later on, he was given an early release of ten years after serving as a dog trainer for eight years; no doubt the dog training benefitted him in the eyes of the parole officers. He also said that working with the dogs changed him for the good.

"Tell me what happens in prison?" I curiously asked.

After taking a deep breath, he began. "When you are sentenced to prison for a long time, you immediately lose all sense of your former identity, your self-esteem and any pride you might have had. Since my sentence was for twenty, I knew this would be too long to expect my wife to wait for me so I also knew a divorce was imminent. Along with this loss, I also knew I would lose my children…I simply lost everything."

All I could say was, "Wow!" and sadly shake my head, though I knew there was no way I could really understand what he had gone through.

"Did working with the dogs help?"

"In a big, big way," he said, smiling.

"You see, suddenly the dogs arrived and were with you 24/7. The poor things were petrified, in lousy physical condition and would give no eye contact. Remember, these animals came from an animal shelter and this was their last chance. And they were in as bad of a condition as I was."

"What did you learn from training the dogs?"

Smiling again, he said, "Everything—like respect and responsibility. But what became clear very quickly was that my self-esteem became intimately connected with the animal's esteem, and the more the dogs learned, the better *their* self-esteem."

"I had never thought of that before," I said. "How in the world did you come to this insight?"

"It was like the dog and I had an unspoken bond right from the start. We both knew that our lives had become intertwined.

"I'm not sure I could describe how. What I do know was that the dog quickly sensed that I was his only hope. What I didn't know until later...the dog was my only hope, also."

On the way out of the restaurant, we ran into the person who had started and still heads up Freedom Dog Service. His respect for her was obvious, and hers for him. Then I was invited to an awards meeting. They both suggested I would be able to better see exactly what the Freedom Dog Service was all about.

His supervisor then explained that the organization changed its focus in 2009 because of all the injured veterans returning from Iraq and Afghanistan. Now its major emphasis would be upon matching deserving disabled veterans with a trained service dog companion. She emphasized that Freedom Dog Service used only "positive reinforcement" in their training.

***

After driving off, my mind began spinning. Maybe, just maybe, our world is finally opening to the possibility that every living thing on this planet of ours has a purpose and was put here to add value. Be it dog or broken man, we can all become healed and useful once again. I recalled a line from the movie, **Seabiscuit**, *"You don't throw away a horse just because he's a little banged up."*

One day the absurdity of the almost universal human belief in the *slavery of animals* will be palpable. We shall then have discovered our souls and become worthier of sharing this planet with them.

—Martin Luther King, Jr.
Clergyman and human rights advocate
(1929–1968)

HE ANIMAL PICTURED ABOVE IS called a coati.

Similar to a raccoon, these furry little creatures are found in the southern United States and Mexico. They are quite beautiful, but very shy.

My wife and I have some friends who live in Cancun, Mexico and knew I was writing a book about animals exhibiting traits from which we humans could learn. Our dear friend, Rosa Maria Lopez Moreno, sent me this email and I'm going to write down this story just as she e-mailed it to me.

"Hi, Ernie, I am so impressed by the beauty we hardly ever see or notice. Now that you are writing about animals, just an hour ago, my dear cousin-in-law, who lives here in Cancun too, told me during dinner about a family of coatis.

"She said she noticed from her balcony that the whole family was eating fruit off of a giant tree she has in her garden. These animals rarely come near the houses even though they live all around us in the mangrove.

"There was a mom, dad and three little ones. When her husband went outside to the garden to have a closer look, all the coatis ran along a branch that was close to the wall that separated the house from the mangrove. Running as fast as they could and in a row, the biggest one led (we assumed it was the father), followed by the little ones. They all made the jump from the branch to the fence...all except the last one, the littlest one, whose legs must not have been long enough or strong enough to reach the wall and fell, splat, onto the ground.

"Nobody moved, not even the coatis' mom, who nervously watched everything from the tree. The pup quickly got up off the ground and without thinking, ran up the tree again, made the jump, only to fall a second time. Three times he fell and three times he repeated the jump. The father stayed all this time while the mother watched from the top of the tree. Only after the pup's fourth attempt did he make it to the fence and it was then that the mother could flee and also jump onto the fence. Then they all disappeared into the thick mangroves.

"My cousin, Sylvia, and her husband wanted to cry in amazement over the love, commitment, support and courage the parents displayed by not abandoning their little one, even though I am guessing that they had to have been experiencing great fear. *It made them reflect on all of the humans in our world who mistreat their own children, much less ever do anything so brave."*

Compassion for animals is intimately connected with goodness of character; and it may be confidently asserted that he who is cruel to animals cannot be a good man.

—Arthur Schopenhauer
German philosopher
(1788–1860)

A SECOND LESSON IN OVERCOMING ADVERSITY

IF YOU HADN'T ALREADY GUESSED, these are pictures of hedgehogs. The name of the one on the left is Lt. General Biggs, while the one on the right is named Wilma.

I Googled them and found that:

- Hedgehogs are small, nocturnal mammals that are covered in spines which are used for their defense. If attacked, they will curl up in a ball so all that shows is the sharp spines. Very few predators want to mess with them.
- They feed on insects, snails, frogs, and snakes and love melons and berries. They are also effective at pest control in gardens and can eat up to 200 grams or almost one-half of a pound of insects each night.

As many animals as I have known, I had never had the pleasure of coming face-to-face with a real live hedgehog—not in a zoo or out in the wild.

One of the joys of life is the little surprises that are bestowed upon us, something totally unexpected and wonderful—like this hedgehog Max and I got to meet at a conference. We were talking before the meeting began when I looked over and saw a strange critter. I must have seen one in a book before because I immediately said its name to myself. Walking directly over to where this little cutie was being held by a man, I introduced myself and discovered that the man's name was Z.G. Standing Bear. While petting the spiny little creature, he told me that he had started the International Hedgehog Society and that their purpose was to rescue injured hedgehogs and help others to know how to care for them.

The hedgehog below and on the left is named Lolita Rose and the one on the right is King Walter the Wise.

Now look at the picture of the hedgehog just below this sentence.

See how long this one is? Her name is Buttercup and she has a disease of the spine. But despite her condition, she does not seem to mind it one little bit. With never a thought of feeling sorry for herself, she is so active and energetic that Z.G. Standing Bear entered her into a hedgehog competition. To his amazement, Buttercup captured the gold medal. One of the spectators who had grown quite fond of Buttercup said, "I guess she doesn't know she's disabled."

Once again, Max and I experienced firsthand our animal friends exhibiting this intriguing trait of *not feeling sorry for themselves when injured*. Most, if not all, animals possess this outlook, this attitude about facing the difficulties that everyone encounters during life.

Albert Einstein wrote later, "One of the greatest secrets in all of life...is that *every* adversity brings with it a gift."

Why do we humans wail and moan about life's difficulties rather than to stop focusing on our misfortune and move on with our life? The longer I live, the more truth I see in Einstein's quote and the more I try to remember this powerful teaching lesson these animals provide to us. They are, in a sense, much more evolved in some ways than we egotistical humans will ever be.

By the way, I read Z.G. Standing Bear's charming little book titled, ***THE GATHERING: Secretly Saving the World***. It is about hedgehogs and how they join forces to save our world. I'm sixty-three years old and I loved it. I will also love reading it to my brand new granddaughter when she gets a bit older.

While teaching a Sunday school class on animals, the teacher stated that leopards cannot change their spots. One little girl quickly raised her hand and contradicted the teacher by saying, "Of course leopards can change their spots...if they don't like the spot they're in, they can move to another spot."

God sleeps in a stone, dreams in a flower, moves in an *animal* and wakes in man.

—Unknown

A CHICKEN NAMED VALERIE

I'VE GOT TO TELL YOU, this story really cracked me up. It is also *the* only story I have ever heard about a human having a chicken for a pet, or in this case a chicken adopting a human.

My wife is an award-winning author and great motivational speaker. As a flight attendant with a major airline, she met another attendant named Patty P. Somewhere along in the relationship, Patty happened to mention to me that she had a pet chicken.

"What?" I said a bit stunned.

"Oh yeah," she said smiling, "I have a real live pet chicken named Valerie, who acts more like a dog than a chicken." Then she began her tale, which I am going to let Patty tell you in her own words.

***

Valerie came to live at Luce Haven Lodge as a condemned hen—condemned because no one, especially the other chickens, liked her. My neighbors, Bob and Paula, had been at their normal Sunday church services where the subject of chickens apparently came up during their social time with fellow parishioners. A couple there mentioned having an "anti-social hen" that didn't lay eggs or associate with the other hens. They mentioned that Bob and Paula could have her for Sunday dinner.

In talking with Paula some days later, she mentioned that if I heard anything strange, they had a chicken in the horse trailer. My response was, "Exactly WHY do we have a chicken in the horse trailer?" She explained how they came to bring her home, and for whatever reason promptly named her Valerie.

A neighbor dropped in one afternoon while we were cleaning up from a yard sale. The talk turned to chickens. He asked me if I'd ever made a chicken go to sleep. Having been a farm girl in years past, I told him I'd only raised them for eggs and our dinner table. He asked me to pick her up with my hands "hugging" her where her wings were. He tucked her little head under a wing, and instructed me to swing her back and forth. Feeling a little silly, standing in the yard swinging a chicken back and forth, I told him I'd get even if he was playing a joke.

Shortly, I felt her body relaxing, her legs were completely dangling below her, and the man said I should set her on the ground. As I did, she popped her head out of her wing, and away she went doing her chicken business. Later in the day, as we were finishing our chores, I grabbed her again, flipped her over on her back much like cradling a baby, feet upward, and swung her side to side. She quickly relaxed so completely, her head was hanging down, completely limp. I laid her on the grass still upside down in the same position, looking as if she'd passed on, for five minutes or more. Then she opened one eye, and then the other, flipped over on her feet and went about her business. We all got a good laugh over it and ended our day.

The next afternoon, after taking a nice motorcycle ride, I arrived home and began washing the road dust off before putting my bike away. Valerie was right under my feet the whole time I was at the water hydrant. As I reached the point of drying and polishing the chrome, just to keep from stepping on her, I picked her up and set her on the toy stuffed dog I had secured on the motorcycle's back seat.

With a bungee cord keeping the mascot securely on my rear luggage rack, he didn't protest having a hen on his head. For her part, Valerie seemed to think she was pretty hot stuff, and was very verbal in her little hen way, and seemed to adopt a bit of "attitude" right then and there. I finished polishing the chrome, the sun was getting lower, and she stayed right there. I assumed that she would be frightened and fly off as soon as I started the engine.

Wrong! She never moved, even when I backed the bike back out of the space, deciding to go down our winding driveway to see how she would react. She used her wings for balance as we wound our way toward the main road. We reached the road. I turned right toward the little town of Conifer.

Wanting to keep her safe, I rode pretty slowly, never over thirty-five mph. Naturally many people came upon us as they headed back to Denver after their day in the mountains. We received a few odd looks, many grins and thumbs up, and a totally dumbfounded trio of bikers on the side of the road as we passed by. But, from that afternoon on, it was as if I had been adopted by her; I became HER human.

Anytime I took the motorcycle cover off, she would be right there under my feet, much like an enthusiastic pooch wanting to jump in the truck for a ride! I had to shoo her away from my convertible more than once as I headed to the airport to work filled with pangs of guilt as to whether I had given her enough attention. She would run after me as I roamed the mountain hiking, going to the mailbox, whatever I did, she tried to do!

Sadly, during the following late spring to early summer, she was out in the yard chasing bugs and enjoying the day, and was apparently taken by a wild animal who didn't follow the nocturnal hunting rule. Now, we all still miss her so much. She had become a part of our family…this chicken who had adopted a human—me.

"Wow!" I said. "What can you say about a story like this?" Max was laughing.

But then his face turned serious. "Ernie, this story may prove something of great significance—that all animals have varying degrees of intelligence." Resuming his laughter, he added, "Even a chicken!"

If you wish to see more of this story, go to YouTube and type in "bikerchickspatty."

The best things about animals are that they don't talk much.

—THORNTON WILDER

AMERICAN PLAYWRIGHT AND NOVELIST

(1897–1975)

ESFP
(Extra Sensory Feline Perception)

"ERNIE, I WAS READING the *Denver Post* newspaper yesterday morning and came across something interesting."

Max and I were having coffee and orange scones at a Paneras. He continued, "One of the most potentially explosive new fields of learning that could launch our society into a brave and better new world is the area of *animal-human bonding*."

In deep thought, he asked, "Do you remember that old Star Trek movie about a gigantic machine that was floating in space and was going to destroy our planet unless it received a special message from…a humpback whale? The author of this script created this story about a machine from a much advanced society. He intuitively sensed that animals hold many vital keys to our planet's expanding consciousness.

"Well, the University of Denver is making some of the greatest new advances in this area of the Human-Animal Bond. The discoveries are so far-reaching that they could actually reshape law enforcement, social work, and domestic violence."

I remembered conversations with Jodi and Paul Messenich of Zuma's Horse Rescue when they repeatedly referred to Phil Tedeschi at the University of Denver. "He's one of the main forces in this new field of the animal-human connection," Jodi had said. "You really ought to contact him."

So we decided to set up a meeting. Immediately liking his voice over the telephone (it held no pretense whatsoever), agreed to meet in his office.

Philip Tedeschi is an associate clinical professor and the clinical director of the Institute for Human-Animal Connection, both within the purview of the University of Denver's Graduate School of Social Work. He has also been an instructor in Outward Bound and has focused primarily upon *non-traditional* therapeutic approaches (since the traditional approaches have had so little success, he says).

One of the articles that Max and I read was titled, "A Calming Presence," and was written for the magazine, *CAT FANCY,* May 2009 issue. He explains:

"Our soldiers returning from war sometimes experienced PTSD (Post Traumatic Stress Disorder), which can create a high degree of anxiety. This in turn affects everything from difficulty making friends to holding down a job. It can cause people to be hyper-vigilant and over-reactive to their environment. It is very disabling and very exhausting to have to live like this.

"We have discovered that *cats* can be trained to recognize when a veteran starts going into PTSD; the cat is somehow able to detect subtle changes in both the veteran's current environment *and* what is going on inside him/her. They then can perform such *'highly technical' stress reducing techniques* as climbing onto the veteran's shoulder and nibbling or licking their ear."

Tedeschi continued, "Cats have proven they possess a special characteristic for this particular problem—that of having the unique ability to sense the onset of PTSD before it arrives."

Max and I discussed what we had learned from our meeting.

"Max, had you ever heard of a cat being able to do such a thing?"

"Nope. I had no idea that these animals were impacting the world so much," Max sighed in wonderment. "And these talents are the one's we are just now becoming aware of. Why, my goodness, what other new talents are we going to see that haven't even surfaced yet?"

Until we extend our circle of compassion to all living things, humanity will not find peace.

—Albert Schweitzer
Physician, theologian,
musician and philosopher
(1875–1965)

ANIMAL CRUELTY AND DOMESTIC VIOLENCE

"ERNIE," MAX SAID EXCITEDLY, closing the book in his lap, "I just finished a book by the other person I told you about who does work on the Human-Animal Bond.

"His name is Frank Ascione. He is a professor and American Humane Chair Executive Director for the Institute for Human-Animal Connection there.

"What the fancy title really means is that this guy is leading Denver University's School of Social Work in a groundbreaking new program that explores the ways people and pets are interconnected."

Max was always someone who was fascinating to be around; his enthusiasm was contagious.

"This book of his is fantastic. Titled, *Children and Animals: Exploring the Roots of Kindness,* it focuses on the most singular distinguishing characteristic of a sociopath is *lack of empathy.* And those children who start off in life not possessing this very important trait of empathy often become sociopaths later in life.

"Dr. Ascione discovered that it is in the interactions between animals and children who lack any sense of empathy, that we have a *window of opportunity—childhood*—where we can change the creation of new sociopaths by helping them develop this empathy tool.

"He proves that in regard to acts of cruelty to animals, there is a direct correlation between animal abuse in the household and domestic violence—that there is a link between animals abused by children and those same children being abused by their parents or caretakers."

***

"I guess I should borrow it and read it next, huh, Max?"

Max's face suddenly reflected an unusual seriousness.

"What's wrong, Max?"

"Ernie, I just had the weirdest thought. Ironically, these animals are helping to heal our planet even when that aid comes about by showing us that signs of cruelty to animals may point to a potential sociopathic tendency in children."

"I hadn't looked at it like that before, but you're right. Animals have become indispensable to us."

Until one has loved an animal, a part of one's soul remains unawakened.

—Anatole France
French Writer
(1844–1924)

A DOG'S DIARY vs. A CAT'S DIARY

XCERPTS FROM A DOG'S DIARY

Day number 180

8:00 am—Wow! Dog food! My favorite!

9:30 am—Oh boy! A car ride! My favorite!

9:40 am—Wow! A walk! My favorite!

10:30 am—Oh boy! A car ride! My favorite!

11:30 am—Wow! Dog food! My favorite!

12:00 noon—Oh boy! The kids! My favorite!

1:00 pm—Oh boy! The yard! My favorite!

4:00 pm—Yea! The kids! My favorite!

5:00 pm—Oh boy! Dog food! My favorite!

5:30 pm—Wow! Dad's home! My favorite!

10:00 pm—Oh boy! Time to go to sleep on the bed! My favorite!

Day number 181

(The same as day number 180)

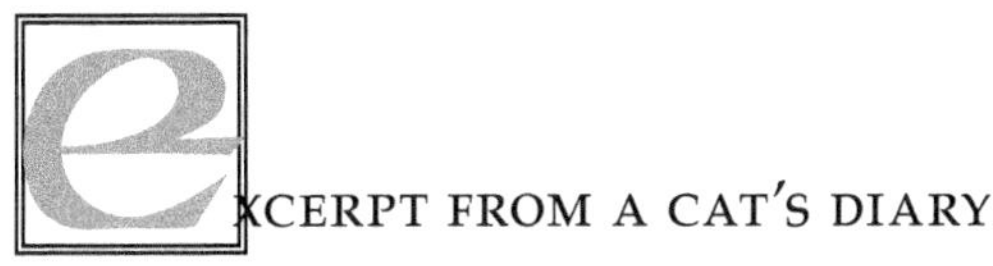

EXCERPT FROM A CAT'S DIARY

DAY 752—My evil captors continue to tease me with strange little dangling objects. They dine richly on fresh meat, while I am forced to eat dry cereal. The only thing that keeps me going is the hope of escape, and the mild satisfaction I get from ruining the occasional piece of furniture...Tomorrow I may defecate in another plant box.

DAY 761—Today my attempt to kill my captors by weaving around their feet while they are walking almost succeeded. I must try this at the top of the stairs. In an attempt to disgust and repulse these vile oppressors, I once again induced myself to vomit on their favorite chair...must try this on their bed.

DAY 765—I decapitated a large rat and brought them the headless body in an attempt to make them aware of what I am capable of, and to try to strike fear into their hearts. They only smiled and patted me and told what a good little cat I was...This is not working according to my planning.

DAY 768—I am finally aware of how sadistic they are. For no good reason I was chosen for the water torture. They even used a burning foamy chemical called "shampoo." What sick minds could invent such a poison? I am wondering if I will die from it. My only consolation is the piece of thumb I was able to tear from their hand...

The time will come when
men such as I will look
upon the murder of animals
as they now look upon
the murder of men.

—Leonardo Da Vinci
Painter, sculptor, architect,
mathematician
(1452–1519)

FINNEGAN THE SQUIRREL

I INCLUDED THIS STORY in my earlier book, ***CONNECTED BY THE SOUL: Oh, the Oneness of Us All***. Because so many readers liked it so much, I decided to also include it in this book.

Now we all know that some animals do not naturally get along. We might even say that some animals are natural born enemies…like dogs and squirrels, right?

Wrong. Take a gander at the pictures below. As for the story itself, I got it directly from the *horse's mouth*.

Whenever there is an animal in need, friends and strangers know to bring them to Debby Cantlon. One day someone brought her a newborn squirrel that had fallen out of a tree. Debby, who eventually released Finnegan back into the woods, initially bottle-fed the tiny baby squirrel. Do notice how Finnegan gripped the little bottle.

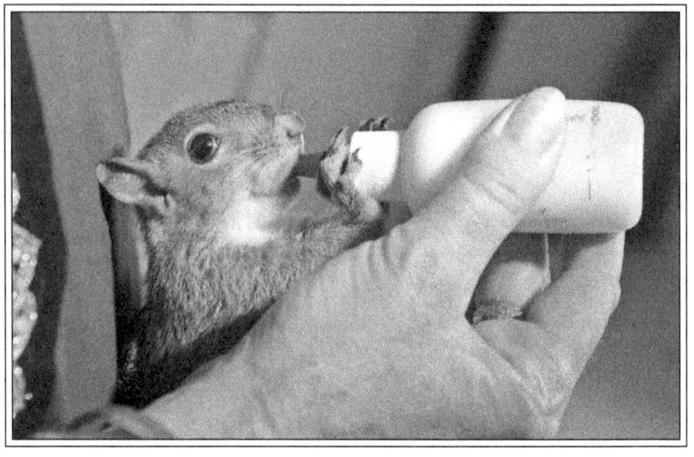

After caring for him for awhile, she soon discovered that she would have help from a most unlikely source—her pregnant Papillion dog, Mademoiselle Giselle.

Finnegan was asleep in a homemade nest snuggled up in a cage just two days before Giselle was to deliver her puppies.

And then something most strange occurred. Debby had left for errands only to find upon her return the squirrel's kennel was missing! She soon discovered it had been moved into the same room as her pregnant dog. Debby lugged the large case back to its original place in another room.

Later, upon returning from another errand, she found the kennel had been moved again! Since no one else had been home, the only possibility was that the dog must be the mysterious culprit who kept dragging it back next to her birthing bed. This time Debby decided to leave it there.

Soon after the puppies were born, Debby was awakened by Giselle's scratching on Finnegan's kennel. Finally understanding, Debbie opened his door and watched as the new mother allowed Finnegan to nurse alongside her new puppies.

As you can see, Finnegan and his new littermates, five Papillion puppies, get along quite well.

But let me ask a most pertinent question. How can two natural born enemies, dogs and squirrels, ever get along and live with one another? How could this ever happen?

Maybe the lesson our whole world might learn from this situation is that we all can *learn to get along with one another*...regardless of what "species" or "race" or "culture" we come from—that we were all put on this planet together for this purpose of overcoming our differences and learning to recognize our oneness.

World Peace...what a concept!

Human beings have a kind of optical illusion. We see ourselves as separate rather than part of the whole.

—Albert Einstein
from *Oh, the Oneness of Us All,*
by Ernie Carwile

Teaching a child not to step on a caterpillar is as valuable to the child as it is to the caterpillar.

—BRADLEY MILLAR
ANIMAL ADVOCATE

A REGRET THAT WILL LAST A LIFETIME

A WHILE BACK, I began dating a lady who later became my wife and eventually the mother of our daughter.

She had a young husky, who was gorgeous, but as she said, "Not too bright and a bit off the wall." Being a little too rambunctious, "Yuri" sometimes just got on your nerves. One time, however, when my wife wasn't in the room, I gently kneed him in the chest to keep him from jumping up on me. It wasn't too long after that I realized that after the kneeing, Yuri had not jumped up even once and ergo, that this dog was no dummy after all.

Since I had grown up with Labradors, I tactfully suggested to her that perhaps we could get rid of Yuri so we could get a Labrador puppy. After thinking over the proposition, she finally admitted that she couldn't just give Yuri to someone else.

Accepting my fate, I then suggested we should start treating Yuri with more respect since he was going to be with us for a long while. Little did I know the amazing turnaround that was about to take place; as we treated Yuri with more respect, this animal calmed down and started doing whatever we asked of him. It was just phenomenal to see this. He became a great pet and friend.

We had many adventures, Yuri and I, from jogging every morning to mountain hikes and exploring. He taught me so much about acceptance and unconditional loving and humor.

He also suffered from epileptic seizures. Whenever the onset of one appeared, Yuri would begin crawling over to me. I would then pet him and tell him over and over again that he "was a great hunter and tougher than all the other dogs." He seemed to like this because we repeated this scenario many times. After each seizure, he would usually give me a big lick and then carry on like nothing had happened.

Our relationship extended into the arena of humor, and Yuri excelled. One of his favorite tricks came whenever I made the bed. As I was making it, I began to notice Yuri peeking around the wall. Just as I pulled up the bedspread cover signaling that I was almost through, he would run into the bedroom, jump on the bed and then deliberately twist the cover as he leapt off. I would, of course, pretend that I was angry and chase him all around the house. I could almost hear him laughing.

Then, what happens to all of our pets way too soon, he became old with all the indignities that come with it: he was no longer the king, nor the toughest dog, nor the most beautiful dog anymore, and you could see in his eyes the shame and lack of respect the world had now saddled upon him.

Just shortly before we had to put Yuri down, he developed incontinence (loss of bladder control). We discovered this one night while watching television. Yuri suddenly stood up, got a strange, faraway look in his face and peed a real gusher while standing right in front of us. My response was to grab a newspaper, smack him with it and then rub his face in the pee, just like we had done when he was a pup.

The look of shame on his face was crystal clear.

It took me only a short time to remember his age, that incontinence was common and had nothing to do with him being a bad dog. After realizing what I had done, I told him over and over how sorry I was for overreacting, but that earlier look of shame in his eyes was forever burned into my memory.

If only I could have thought faster, if only I hadn't acted like a self-righteous idiot, if only I would not have to relive that one brief episode intermittently throughout the rest of my life, nor remember that stunned and shameful look in the eyes of my dog that had once been a *king*.

Do I think Yuri forgave me? Absolutely! However, the problem was me forgiving myself. You see, *self*-forgiveness is sometimes the most difficult impediment for being able to move on in life, a life lesson I learned the *hard way*, perhaps the optimum way to truly learning anything in this lifetime. Our hardest lessons may be the most powerful and important for us.

I ask people why they have deer heads on their wall. They always say because it's such a beautiful animal...I think my mother is attractive, but I have photographs of her.

—Ellen DeGeneres
Talk Show Host Extraordinaire

ON THE DEATH OF A PET

NOTHING EXPOSES THE WORTH OF a living thing more than its loss in death. And nothing hurts so exquisitely as the loss of a dear, dear pet.

Tally, my caring, wonderful and so accepting, so forgiving yellow Lab, it's been three years and I have not had the courage to yet get another dog. You are still in my heart.

This may be the most difficult element of having a pet; they just don't stay around long enough. But then, how many years would be long enough?

My daughter was the one who broke my shell of denial. "Dad, are you aware of how much panting Tally is doing?" *Yes, I mean no, I mean…I guess that I had repressed her showing signs of decline. On some level of consciousness I'm sure I knew but still desperately hoped the medications were doing their job, but I guess…*

"Dad, I know how much you love Tally and she loves you back, but it isn't right to keep her alive for your sake alone." *Out of the mouths of babes, I thought to myself.*

Actually, this is so painful that I'm going to let my wife tell the story from her perspective.

I didn't have pets growing up. Not a one, nor do I remember any friends having animals either. I'm sure some people did in our little town of Webster, South Dakota, but they were just not common in the homes of the people I knew.

When I had children, for one of my sons, pets became very important. He *needed* a dog and asked for one every single day for over a year. "Good morning, Mom. Can I have a dog today?" When I finally agreed, there wasn't a happier boy in the world. Sadly, that same son now grown has lost four precious dogs way too early in life and when each dog died, a little bit of my son died with it. He still insists, however, that he will always have a dog in his life—that pain is part of the loving process.

How well I came to understand the wisdom my son proposed for now I am married to a man who loves animals more than anyone I've ever known. He told me right up front that animals are more trustworthy than most people and they love you even when you don't deserve it. It took me awhile to come to this realization, but now...I'm there.

When I had my first date with Ernie, before we said goodbye in the parking lot of the restaurant, he introduced me to his dog, Tally. She was waiting patiently in the back seat of his car. Before the introductions, Ernie gave Tally a small sample of the delicious meal we had just consumed. He *always* gave Tally a taste of what he had eaten. "Sometimes," as Ernie said, "Tally is a Mexican dog, sometimes she's Italian...she's not fussy." Tally was nearly eight years old then—nearly in her Golden Years, and whoever said that hadn't reached those later years. For dogs it comes faster than for we humans, usually. But Tally had such heart! We bonded, Tally and I. She had the sweetest disposition. Maybe all dogs do. I didn't know that then.

As the years passed, Tally began having more and more trouble getting up the steps to our front door or getting into the back seat of the car. I would give her encouragement saying, "Oh, Tally. It's okay. I'll help"—something like that, but not Ernie. He always spoke words of encouragement to her. He'd lift her up and tell what a great dog she was. He always tried to downplay her malady and emphasized her greatness—her spirit.

On one morning, after a weekend away, Ernie's daughter Kate (who'd stayed the weekend with Tally) had a talk with her Dad. "Dad, I think it's time. Tally is really having trouble…" There, it was out. I know Ernie had many long talks with Tally on this topic. "She'll tell me when it's time," Ernie always said, but he somehow *forgot to listen*.

So we planned the event. We researched and found a female veterinarian that specialized in euthanizing dogs in the home. Several phone conversations later, she was at our door. A small, very gentle woman arrived. We knew she'd be leaving with our Tally.

Just prior to her arrival, we had a great big picnic on our living room floor; Ernie, his daughter Kate, Tally and I. We all loved food and took great pleasure in partaking of it. Let me assure you that Tally fit right in. That final day she had all she wanted of a great big submarine sandwich, chips and chocolate chip cookies, one of her many favorites. It was like a Last Supper and I wondered if Tally knew.

Our daughter chose to leave before the kind woman came. Tally had been her *sister* since she was a young girl. She hugged and gave Tally big kisses before she said her final goodbye, then ran out of the room crying.

The woman came well equipped. She first talked with Tally. She gave her some of her own treats she had brought and talked softly and gently all the while reassuring her that everything was going to be alright.

She put down a soft blanket for Tally to lie on. We joined them on the floor. It truly was most peaceful. I thought then as I continue to do today, *wouldn't it be lovely if we could do this for our human loved ones?*

In just a short time, Tally went from our being a beautiful yellow Lab to our *angel*. It wasn't awful. She just went to sleep. The woman stayed right there with us, encouraging our tears until Tally was gone, and then with the help of Ernie, they carried Tally to the back of her vehicle.

Then tears flowed, but not for Tally. Tally was no longer in pain. It's never about the *creature* leaving us. It's about the hole they leave in our hearts and lives.

Tally was a *great spirit*. Ernie told her that often. And yes, we talk about her often, think of her fondly and still have pictures of her around our home. Her dog body isn't with us anymore, but her spirit lives on. Mary Carwile

RAINBOW BRIDGE

IF YOU ARE READING THIS BOOK, it is highly likely that you have animals now and probably have gone through the death process before. There is a fable about dying pets that you may have heard before. It's called the *Rainbow Bridge* and even if you have heard it before, it's worth reading again.

Just this side of heaven is a place called Rainbow Bridge.
When an animal dies that has been especially close to someone here,
That pet goes to Rainbow Bridge.
There are meadows and hills for our special friends
So they can run and play together.
There is plenty of food and water and sunshine
And our friends are warm and comfortable.

All the animals who have been ill and old are
restored to health and vigor again,
Just as we remember them in our dreams of days
and times gone by.
The animals are happy and content, except for
one thing;
They each miss someone very special to them,
who had to be left behind.
They all run and play together, but the day comes
When one suddenly stops and looks off into the
distance.
His bright eyes are intent; his eager body begins
to quiver.
Suddenly he begins to run from the group,
Flying over the green grass,
His legs carry him faster and faster.
You have been spotted and when you and your
special friend finally
Meet, you cling together in joyous reunion,
Never to be parted again.
Happy kisses rain upon your face;
Your hands again caress the beloved head,
And you look once more into the trusting eyes of
your pet,

So long gone from your life
But never absent from your heart.
Then you cross Rainbow Bridge together…

DEDICATED TO TALLY O'MALLY
(Talisker from the Isle of Sky)
WITH GREAT LOVE AND APPRECIATION
FOR ALL THAT YOU TAUGHT ME

ANGELS IN DISGUISE

An angel in disguise,
your form surprised me so.
There were no wings, nor loftiness,
only a cold little nose.

The Master was I,
but who could tell.
You secretly taught me,
lifted me out of my hell.

You forgave my anger and moodiness,
my sharp tongue too.
Always there beside me,
especially when blue.

How did I miss this,
your stature so true?
A loyalty too rare,
a love that only grew.

And now you're gone so completely,
in a blink of time you left.
Leaving my heart empty,
utterly bereft.

Finally understanding who you were,
my whole perception I must revise.
For you were always here with me,
an angel in disguise.

—Ernie Carwile

Dogs have given us their absolute all. We are the center of their universe. We are the focus of their love and faith and trust. They serve us in return for scraps. It is without a doubt the best deal man has ever made.

—Roger Caras
American Wildlife Photographer

SOME FINAL THOUGHTS

SELDOM DO I FIND MYSELF at a loss for words, but after arriving at the end of this book I am unable to adequately describe the newly enhanced respect I have developed for animals during its writing.

Certainly I began this journey as someone who absolutely and unreservedly loves and relates to animals. We, Max and I, ended up enlightened after discovering more of the multi-faceted abilities these gifted animals possess.

Please don't misunderstand me, not all animals are gifted, nor are they always nice, just like all people aren't. What I am trying to strongly convey though is that a very many of them seem to have a purpose in being here, and that *purpose is to teach us.*

We've all heard the term "dumb animal" and I know it came from Anna Sewell, the author of *Black Beauty* way back in 1877, when she wrote, "We call them dumb animals...for they cannot tell us how they feel, but they do not suffer less because they have no words." The words also instantly remind us of the wonderful organization called The Dumb Friends League. It joins such other animal organizations as the ASPCA, American Humane Association, Delta Society, PETA, the Humane Society, animal shelters, animal sanctuaries, and the Animal Cruelty Society, all of which have expended great time, love and money to saving and protecting the animals with which we share our planet.

But, I've got to admit that most animals are anything but dumb.

St. Francis of Assisi, the Patron Saint of Animals, so loved the birds, animals and little creatures that they could sense his love and would gather around him, congregating at his feet. He would speak to them of their Creator. He called them "little brothers and sisters," and still today, over eight hundred years since his death, he stands as our patron saint guiding us on how to treat and interact with these wonderful, amazing God-created beings.

So, the next time you happen upon an animal (not a dangerous one), you might just wish to not simply ignore it; instead, try to making eye contact, then mind-communicate. If you are like me, you might be totally surprised as to the outcome. These creatures have amazing lessons for us humans. I know I am a better man having gotten to know some of them.

And oh, if you can afford to, please donate to as many of the organizations mentioned at the end of the book as you can afford...Ernie

What if...just what if animals were not the "dumb" friends we had once thought them to be, but were actually angels... angels in disguise...sent here to be our teachers?

Bark Less.
Wag More.

**WANT TO
ORDER MORE COPIES?**

**WANT TO
ORDER THE FIRST EIGHT
COMPLETED BOOKS IN THE
MAXWELL WINSTON STONE SERIES?**

**GO TO
WWW.ERNIECARWILE.COM**

DONATIONS/CONTACTS

IF YOU SO DESIRE, **you can make donations to some fine organizations at the following web sites:**

1. The stories about Mandy and Chaco AND Tami and Dare—www.AmericanHumaneAAT.org.
2. Colorado Horse Rescue—www.chr.org.
3. Zuma Rescue Ranch—www.zumarescueranch.com.
4. Harrison Memorial Animal Hospital—www.cvmf.com.
5. University of Denver—www.humananimalconnection.org
6. Freedom Dog Service (matches veterans with a service dog)—www.fdr.com.

7. Animal Whisperer Joyce Leake—www.AnimalUniversity.com.
8. Equine psychotherapist, Suzanne Carter—www.UnityWholenessCenter.com.

Ernie Carwile was born in Munich, Germany and has lived throughout the world. He is a graduate of the University of Missouri and the Iliff School of Theology in Denver, Colorado. After high school he sold cemetery plots door-to-door in Hannibal, Missouri, and while attending college, he drove trucks for Peabody Coal Mine. Mr. Carwile has been an Air Force Officer, heavyweight boxer, and a Methodist and Congregational minister.

As a celebrated author and master storyteller, Carwile has been featured extensively in the national media including *Good Morning America*, *Inside Edition*, *CNN* and the *Associated Press*. His books have received Endorsements/Thank You's from the President of the United States and twelve U. S. Governors.

He lives in Denver, Colorado with his award-winning author and wife, Mary Catherine Carwile.

www.ingramcontent.com/pod-product-compliance
Lightning Source LLC
La Vergne TN
LVHW050629100826
845148LV00011B/1795

* 9 7 8 0 9 7 9 6 1 7 6 4 5 *